Robert Kelley Weeks

Twenty Poems

Robert Kelley Weeks

Twenty Poems

ISBN/EAN: 9783744710459

Printed in Europe, USA, Canada, Australia, Japan

Cover: Foto ©Thomas Meinert / pixelio.de

More available books at **www.hansebooks.com**

TWENTY POEMS

BY

R. K. WEEKS

NEW YORK
HENRY HOLT AND COMPANY
1876

Copyright.
ROBERT KELLEY WEEKS
1876.

CONTENTS.

MISCELLANEOUS PIECES.

	Page.
On the River	3
On the Bridge	5
After Twilight	7
Anadyomene	9
Urania	11
The Quiet Moon	12
A Midsummer Night's Dream	13
In September	19
A Sunset in November	20
A Cloudy Day	23
Before the Snow	25
A Snow Shower in April	26
An Old Play	27
Song	32
Love's Incapacity	33
On the Shore	34

A Hill-Top	35
A Climber	36
Andromeda's Escape	41

BALLADS.

How Roland Blew the Horn	107
Gudrun	125
A Song for Lexington	165

MISCELLANEOUS PIECES.

POEMS.

ON THE RIVER.

BETWEEN green fields and wooded heights
   The river stretched at ease;
The starry points, the dazzling lights
   Struck from it by the breeze;

The wavering smoke, that floats, that trails,
   The rippling flags that fly,
The glistening prows, the sunny sails
   Of boats that pass me by;

The gulls that flying here and there
   Now darken and now gleam;
The clouds that melt upon the air,
   Like snow on some slow stream;

Awhile I watch them dreamily,
And then I hear once more
The winds that search infinity,
The waves that beat the shore.

ON THE BRIDGE.

TOWARD the mysterious lights that seem
   To lure it with a smile,
Green between greener fields the stream
   Winds westward many a mile;

The west wind with a lingering hold,
   Voluptuously grave,
Stays every hollow, touched with gold,
   Of every little wave;

The light oars dip and drip and shine,
   The river grasses sway,
The foam-bells in a glimmering line
   Mingle and melt away;

Athwart the sunset, flying low,
    Through light from dark to dark,
A few belated swallows show
    Like whirling leaves; and hark!—

'Tis but the cricket's earthy song,
    The wind's, the water's sigh,
That mingling deepen and prolong
    The silence of the sky.

AFTER TWILIGHT.

1.

STRAIGHT from the golden west serene
   It seemed to come, the restless breeze,
That bent, that lifted, ill at ease,
The massy foliage, darkly green,
Of June's voluptuous apple-trees;

2.

Like great uneven waves they seemed,
Forever breaking with a sigh
'Gainst that unclouded solemn sky,
Whose mingling hues so softly gleamed,
So silently began to die.

3.

The mellow gold, the tender green,
Slow dying, died away at last,
Once more the sky but as a vast
Unquestionable vault was seen,
Its gentler influence overpast.

4.

But still the western breezes blow,
And still the tree-tops sway and sigh ;
All night I hear them where I lie,
Wierd wandering sounds that come and go,
That come and go, and never die.

ANADYOMENE.

THE passionate first flush
  Of that great sunset came,
And vanished, like a rush
Of self-consuming flame;

But deep within the west,
Long lived the afterglow,
And on the water's breast
Slow heaving to and fro;

And where the lower blue
Was lost in tender green,
An eager star burst thro'
The palpitating screen;

And darkly whispering went
The wind among the grass,
And o'er the waves, intent
On what should come to pass;

Eastward I turned my eyes
In vague expectancy,
And saw the moon arise
Like Venus from the sea.

URANIA.

1.

IN the sky a pallid gleam
   Follows sunset's rosy glow,
And the clouds that all astream
Passionately coloured so,
Cold and grey and withered seem.

2.

Then the exhausted clouds between,
Faintly smiling, wan and fair,
Twilights lonely star is seen,
Out of deeper depths of air,
Charming with a milder mien.

THE QUIET MOON.

How still the air, how still the stream!
  The elm-trees hardly breathe,
And breathlessly the waters seem
  To linger underneath.

Not clearer on the cloudless air
  The listening tree-tops lie,
Than on the unruffled river there
  That seems another sky.

And through the branches from above,
  And through them from below,
The new moon, hovering like a dove,
  Gleams and forgets to go.

A MIDSUMMER NIGHT'S DREAM.

THE hot, unhappy city
   Oppresses me all day,
But with the stars reviving
   My spirit slips away.

A country road it enters,
   And follows all alone,
Beside the scented meadows
   That were but newly mown;

Beside the streaming corn-fields
   That rustle in the breeze,
Beside the tangled thickets
   Concealing mysteries.

And here and there it crosses
    A brook that sings and shines,
Or whispers in the shadow
    Of overhanging vines.

And here a waveless water
    It smoothly passes by,
With silvery silent lilies
    Unshaded from the sky.

The flower of the elder-berry
    Perfumes the sunny air,
The milk-white honeysuckle's
    Delicious scent is there;

The wild wide-open roses
    Half hide the farmer's wall,
And there the bees are humming
    And there the robins call;

There like a windy blossom
   The yellow-bird goes by,
There floats in dreamy silence
   The mystic butterfly;

There like a gliding shadow,
   The squirrel skims the rail,
There sounds the saucy whistle
   Of the tantalizing quail;

And self-absorbed the crickets
   There, everywhere approve
The seeming-conscious quiet
   Through which the noises move.

Yet, sweet as is the fragrance
   That there the blossoms yield,
And dear as are the noises
   From thicket and from field,

At times another odour
  Is felt obscurely there,
An odour and a murmur
  That die upon the air.

But ever as they vanish
  The heart begins to say,
What is it that I long for,
  More than I have to-day?

A larger space above me,
  A larger space around,
A sense of deeper silence,
  A sense of fuller sound.

Enough, thou sheltered valley,
  Of sky-perplexing trees,
Of mingling lights and shadows,
  Of dreams and reveries;

The road goes on and upward,
   And I go up and on,
And reach the open head-land
   That loves the unshaded sun.

No shadows overcome it,
   But of the birds that range,
And of the clouds forever
   That wander and that change.

There all the breezes gather,
   There all the winds are heard,
There with a sound of waters
   The air is ever stirred.

The sea's incessant waters,
   That sky-ward laugh and play,
That shore-ward rolling whiten
   And scatter into spray,

The hum of their advancing
The thunder of their fall,
The moan of their recoiling
I hear, I see them all :

And all of them including,
To all of them unknown,
See heaven's unruffled silence,
High over and alone.

IN SEPTEMBER.

FEATHERY clouds are few and fair,
   Thistle-down is on the air,
Rippling sunshine on the lake.
Wild grapes scent the sunny brake,
Wild bees murmuring take the ear,
Crickets make the silence dear;
Butterflies float in a dream,
Over all the swallows gleam.
Here and yonder, high and low,
Golden-rod and sunflowers glow,
Here and there a maple flushes,
Sumach reddens, woodbine blushes,
Purple asters bloom and thrive,—
I am glad to be alive!

A SUNSET IN NOVEMBER.

THE leaden slowness of the prostrate clouds,
The dark pre-eminence of naked boughs,
The blind compulsion of the uncertain wind,
The helpless rustling of the withered leaves,
The listless movement of the abandoned waves,
I marked them all, I made them all my own,
To help me to the sunset I foresaw,
And longed for fiercely that November day.

It came at last, I know not how it came,
A clouded fire showed smouldering in the west,
Faded and seemed extinguished. Overhead
The massy clouds, like giants out of dreams

A SUNSET IN NOVEMBER.

Uneasily awaking, rolled apart,
Closed, wavered, opened, with a sudden gleam
Of silvery edges; and then all was changed.
Upsprang the breeze, the waves, the branches
    sprang;
The brown leaves quivered and went by like birds;
The smouldering clouds about the western hills
Upblown rose huddling, and let see the sun—
Red, rayless, half consumed,—beyond the Earth
Slow drawing backward; while around his place
And over him increasing, the new light
Burnt red, intense and glowing, here and there
Veiled with a restless vapour that arose
Confused and formless, like a fiery smoke.
Lower he sank; o'erhead the parted clouds,
Lightened and thinned and stretching them in
    flight,
Flushed and grew crimson; while beyond the lake
Joyous with gold and purple, and beyond

The feathery outlines of the purpling hills,
The open west 'neath mingling green and blue
Was one transparent river of bright gold
That northward slowly paling many a mile,
Round crimson islands and past rosy shores,
Streamed silent, waveless, to where side by side
A nestling cluster of round little clouds
Bloomed opalescent in clear amber air.

A CLOUDY DAY.

ALL day the sun has kept himself concealed,
But not in sullenness. Look overhead,
How beautiful the curtain that he draws,
'Twixt heaven and earth soft floating in mid-air
In imperceptible motion, seeming still!
Irregular, innumerable folds,
With shadowy dimples and soft gleaming lines,
Touched with a fleeting colour that endures
Of opalescent tints on silvery grey;
Most like the interior loveliness of some
Rare shell with pearly lining.

I watch it long:
Its many mingling hues that come and go,
Its mazy lines continually changing,

Its shadowy hollows that keep changing too,
Its flowing grace and its superb expanse,
I watch it long, unasking any more;
And yet—'tis but a transitory curtain,
Drawn by the sun to hide him for a day,
Some secret gladness of his own concealing,
Some rarely opening inner depth of Heaven,
Wherein unseen he glories, safe withdrawn,
In happy god-like loneliness afar.

BEFORE THE SNOW.

A SOFT grey sky, marked here and there
With tangled tracery of bare boughs,
A little far-off fading house,
A blurred blank mass of hills that wear
A thickening veil of lifeless air,
Which no wind comes to rouse.

Insipid silence everywhere;
The waveless waters hardly flow,
In silence labouring flies the crow,
Without a shadow, o'er the bare
Deserted meadows that prepare
To sleep beneath the snow.

A SNOW SHOWER IN APRIL.

AH, how much greener does the grass appear,
    How much more strong and constant does it show,
Contrasting with this transitory snow,
Untimely and yet lovely! Far and near,
Light lying on the meadows, it seems here
Like hoary clover; and there, on the low
Slope of the knoll, white strawberry blossoms grow,
And daisies yonder; while, (through all the year
Sight longed for and remembered) pearly clear
Around me the light snow-flakes falling seem
Like cherry blossoms, that down eddying slow,
Some warm May morning when no breezes blow,
All over the fresh grass-plat softly gleam,
And like the snow-flakes softly disappear.

AN OLD PLAY.

I. *In the Street.*

LIKE a breeze from a garden,
    Made sweet with the scent
O' the fresh blooming lilacs,
    She came and she went.

Pure spirit and vision,
    Felt rather than known,
Fain would I have held her
    And made her my own;

But as the unconscious
    Breeze blesses and goes
So went she, more blessing
    And blest than she knows.

II. *In the Garden.*

WHEN lilacs were in blossom,
    And all the air was sweet,
I saw her standing tip-toe
    Upon a garden-seat.

One hand drew down the clusters,
    The other bent a spray,
Held it a little minute,
    And let it slip away.

Lilacs, your life is lengthened
    But you've missed the very best,
The best brief life of lying
    And dying on her breast!

III. *Till Sunrise.*

AWAY to her, fresh morning breeze!
   Uplift and blow aside
Her cloudy curtain, and with ease
   Approach her undenied.

And lightly kiss her mouth and eyes;
   And lightly lift her hair;
And blow about her where she lies
   This scent that fills the air

Of apple-blossoms sweet, that she
   May, waking, long to know
What newly flowering shrub or tree
   Sweetens the morning so;

And past the cloudy curtain there
    Lean forth perhaps to see,
Sweet, fresh and fair, and unaware
    Be seen herself by me.

IV. *Till Moonrise.*

'TIS long, long after sunset,
    And cloudless is the sky,
Yet strangely faint the stars are,
    And strangely faint am I.

Behind the hiding mountain
    They know the moon is near;
And shining at her window
    Soon will my Love appear!

V. *By the Light o' the Moon.*

THE boughs that bend over,
   The vines that aspire
To be close to your window
   Prevent my desire.

Come forth from them, darling!
   Enough 'tis to bear
That between us be even
   Impalpable air!

SONG.

LIKE a fettered boat that pants and pulls,
   And struggles to be free,
When the wind is up, and the whirling gulls
   Are wild with ecstasy—
   Is my heart apart from thee!

Like a boat that leans, that leaps, that flies,
   That sings along the sea,
With a sunny shower of drops that rise
   And fall melodiously—
   Is my heart, Sweetheart, is my heart,
   Is my heart, approaching thee!

LOVE'S INCAPACITY.

As a pale cloud at morning, when the light
    First overcomes it from the unrisen sun,
Is flushed with rosy colour, but anon
Grows paler yet and paler as it feels
The illimitable loveliness expand
Till very heaven cannot contain it all;—
So I foresaw the sunrise of her soul,
So I looked out and loved her, and at once
Was flushed with rosy hopefulness and joy,
Then felt her beauty's uncontrollable increase,
And paler grew and paler with despair.

ON THE SHORE.

HERE many a time she must have walked,
    The dull sand brightening 'neath her feet,
The cool air quivering as she talked,
    Or laughed, or warbled sweet.

The shifting sand no trace of her,
    No sound the wandering wind retains,
But, breaking where the foot-prints were,
    Loudly the sea complains.

A HILL-TOP.

LITTLE more than a rock nearly bare,
    Rough with lichens grey-green, and a line
Of pale yellow grass here and there,
    A few daisies, a tree, and a vine.

But the woodbine's aglow and astream
    Like a cloud that the sunsetting fires, .
And star-like the still daisies gleam,
    And flame-like the cedar aspires!

A CLIMBER.

To climb and climb for hours and hours,
   O'er rocks and ice and snow,
To see at last the flower of flowers,
   Long sought, unseen till now,

Bruised, bleeding, breathless to attain
   At last the final ledge,
Lean over, look and see it plain,
   Just under the rough edge

Of that ice-worn, frost-splintered rock,
   In that keen upper air,
Where never shepherd seeks his flock,
   A lovely wonder there;

To gaze at it, and love it more
    And more the more 'tis seen,—
Star-like, but blood-red at the core
    With cool green leaves serene ;—

To feel its fragrance like a kiss
    Awake and take the heart,
Its motion like a smile dismiss
    And keep despair apart.

To love it, long for it, to lean
    Far and yet farther still,
With trembling fingers touch the green
    And trembling leaves, and thrill,

And thrilling reach again, and fall
    Whirling to where the slow
Cold mockery glacier rivers crawl
    And waste away below,—

This was his life, this was his fate,
   A hard, long, lonely climb,
A failure;—but he stood elate
   Once in the air sublime!

ANDROMEDA'S ESCAPE.

A DRAMATIC POEM.

[*I hope that no one will mistake this little "Andromeda" for an attempt to imitate a Greek tragedy. The resemblance is only superficial, and it is very superficial indeed, as "the judicious," if any such should chance to look into it, will see at once. There is a Chorus, there is dialogue and there is narrative—all this to give me a chance to tell the story in a mixed form of lyric, dramatic and descriptive verse. But all this (used in the freest way, without regard to any of the peculiarities of the ancient Chorus, and without an attempt to represent either ancient ways of life, or ancient forms of art), all this has been to me only as so much outermost shell, into which, as convenient to my purpose I have poured my own anachronistic composition, preferring to try the experiment of filling up with that cloudy mixture to making believe, after laborious refining, with something clearer perhaps, and perhaps only thinner.*

March, 1874.]

ANDROMEDA'S ESCAPE.

In front of the King's palace just before sunrise.
EUDORA and a Group of Girls.

EUDORA.

ALL's over now, and all but us are gone.

Yet we still linger, loth to go or stay,

Shrinking together, shivering, half-benumbed

In this chill atmosphere of sudden grief,

Like sheep that huddle for a little warmth.

But let us go. Nay, wait, here comes the Queen.

KASSIOPEIA.

Girls, for I cannot rest within the house,

Have ye no word of comfort for me here?

EUDORA.

How can we comfort you, unhappy Queen,

Ourselves so comfortless? For what are words,

The wisest, could we speak them, but a new
Insulting torment to the tortured soul,
Like too much sunlight to the wilting flower?
There is no comfort, unless tears avail
And vain complainings to unload the heart.

KASSIOPEIA.

Whom I should comfort, who should comfort me,
The king, indoors, sits like a man of stone,
Unmoving, speechless, with wide-open eyes,
Not down-cast, nor uplifted nor bedimmed,
But straight before him staring hard and dry;
Nor dare I speak to him, for even now,
Laying my hand upon him where he sat
Low on the couch, he shrank as if from fire,
And when (the old word unwittingly slipped forth)
And when I called him *Father*, gave a laugh!

The Chorus.

We do not weep to see
The sun forsake the sky;
The waning moonlight we
Can watch with tearless eye;
The birds, another home
Desiring, fly afar;
We let them go and come,
We know well where they are:

We know they will return
Nor keep too long away,
The dearer that we yearn
To have them ere we may,
The dearer that they are
So loth to tarry long,
Sun, moon and every star
And every flower and song.

But you, sunlike that warmed
And filled our day with light;
Moonlike that cheered and charmed
And glorified our night;
Bird-like that made us blest
With every happy tone;
Flower-like the loveliest
And sweetest ever known;

But you, withdrawn afar
From all you loved before,
We know not where you are,
Shall see you never more;
Shall nor by night nor day,
Nor soon nor later see,
Gone the well-trodden way
To cold obscurity.

There is no word to say,
Alas! and nought to do,
We know not what to pray
Nor whom to pray it to,
We can but weep as yet,
Distrusting every cure,
Unwilling to forget,
Unable to endure.

    PHINEUS (*Entering as the song ceases.*)

But what is it you weep for or for whom?
Vague rumors of strange troubles bring me
    here
With men-at-arms, attended, if perchance
I may be yet of service; but even now
Nothing for certain do I know of all
The rumoured evils that ye fear or bear.

    KASSIOPEIA.

Nothing is now to fear, too much to bear.

O, Phineus, friend, I have no daughter now,
Andromeda is dead!

PHINEUS.

Impossible!

KASSIOPEIA.

'Tis the impossible that comes to pass.
Do mothers kill the children whom they love
Because they love them? Or, is the reward
Of lovely innocence a shameless death?

PHINEUS.

She tortures me with riddles.   Would to God
Some one would tell me what she means by
  this!

KASSIOPEIA.

And there comes one can tell you; ask of him,
He will not falter, telling you the tale.

But as for me, nought is there in the earth
More hateful to me than to see his face,
Unless indeed it were to hear his voice.

(*As she goes, Moiris, the High Priest, enters.*)

PHINEUS.

You know me, Moiris, I have heard strange tales
Of sudden sorrow come upon this house.
Tell me the truth, and let me know the worst.

MOIRIS.

Not willingly, for I, too, have a heart,
Aye, and have learned by proof as well as proverb,
That oft the unhappy bearer of ill news,
Though innocent, to him who hears them seems
A constant part, if not indeed a cause
Of all the affliction that his words convey.
Unjust, but justice is what men expect!

PHINEUS.

I understand you; but the Queen is gone.

Speak, for I grow impatient of suspense,
And haply yet there may be found a cure,
Or if no cure, the comfort of revenge.

MOIRIS.

Cure there is none, but patiently to bear.
And for revenge, 'tis with a mighty God
And not with mortals you will have to deal.

PHINEUS.

Be plain, be plain!

MOIRIS.

    Something you must have heard
Of all we have suffered from a nameless beast,
Sent us for punishment, that from the sea
Comes inland daily to lay waste and slay:—
According to an oracle's command,
To save a wretched people from despair,
Andromeda, our princess, to the beast
Is this day made an offering, one for all.

PHINEUS.

She *is* dead then? Or is it still to do?

MOIRIS.

This morn ere sunrise taking her away,
My priests and I, we brought her to the shore,
Submissive, uncomplaining, strangely calm;
There, not an hour ago, hard by the place
Where first the monster rises every day,
Fast bound to a rock we left her in the sea,
Alive yet and alone.

PHINEUS.

                Alive, alone
And there she may be yet, alive, alone,
Half dead with terror and unfriendly grief!

MOIRIS.

'Twas so commanded by the oracle.

Phineus.

What set you on to ask the oracle?
What cause for so great anger, whose the blame?

Moiris.

Increasing ravage of our flocks and fields,
Slaughter of folk, and terror, and the wrath
Of terror growing frantic, and the tears
And prayers of helpless sorrow set us on.
The Queen's unheard-of folly was the cause;
Who, finding too much happiness too flat,
Must spice it with impiety, forsooth!
Likening Andromeda—not her's the fault—
To deathless Goddesses; nay, more than that
(Unreasoning love is deadlier oft than hate),
Boasting that altars should be built to her,
And Sacrifice be done, and worship paid.
And now, now, what a sacrifice is done!

Phineus.

The Queen's words had a meaning then, tho' wild;
And yet the innocent must suffer all!

MOIRIS.

Not all, not all; and surely not the worst.
No sense of guiltiness increased her pain,
And all her suffering, and this she knew,
Was for the advantage of the ones she loved.

PHINEUS.

Cold comfort there! But still I have to hear
What happened to the people and the land.

MOIRIS.

You know the road that eastward for a mile
Goes hence declining gently to the shore;
On either side of it what fields of grain,
What vines all orderly, row after row,
What pastures crowded with fair flocks and herds,
What orchards, and what meadow-lands afar,
Stretch right and left to meet the including sky,
The comfortable houses and the barns
With noise of children and with noise of fowls,

And the trim gardens near them with their flowers;—

You have all these, have more than once, perhaps,

Been filled with pleasure at the happy sight;—
Go now and see them! where the heavy grain
Reeled in the breeze or slumbered in the sun,
Undreaming of the sickle; where the fruit
Golden and crimson 'mid the dark green leaves
Of topmost bough and lowest shone and swung,
Or gleamed unhurt among the dewy grass
Of many an orchard: where the wrinkled sheep
Cropped audibly their pasture; where the cows,
Mechanically working tireless jaws,
Lay or stood drowsing; where the children played
I' the meadow with the daisies, or behind
The leaning oxen in the clumsy cart
Went jolting with the harvesters afield;
Where wife or daughter now the farmer's meal,
Fresh gathered from the garden, brought in-doors,

And now a handful of selected flowers—
O, why do I so dwell upon it all?—
When not ten days ago whoever passed
Might gladden looking at such sights as these,
Whoever passes sees a desert now.
For not a day and night were passed away
Since the vain Queen's defiance, when there came
Shaming the light that let the thing be seen,
A grisly horror from the shuddering sea.
Utterly silent, with a sleepy eye,
Loathsome to fascination, slow it crawled
To where a group of children on the shore
Huddling together stood without a cry
Breathlessly staring—And at night it came,
Trampling, defiling, beating down the grain,
Uprooting shade and fruit-trees, tearing vines,
Upturning gardens, poisoning springs and streams,
Devouring cattle, rending them piece-meal,
Strewing their carcases about the fields—
And the next day it came, and of the three

Fishers that saw it there is one alive.
And the next night and the next day and night;
And so for six days, day and night it came
As punctual as the sunrise and the stars,
As tireless as the waters of the sea,
And deadlier than the tempest. Till at last,
The people, first half stupefied, and then
Heroically patient, when they found
No help in patience, and no help in arms,
(What few among the soldiers dared affront
The invulnerable monster, arms and all,
Were torn and trampled shapeless in an hour,)
Grew clamorous and then riotous in their pain,
With proclamation of a new-found law.
Who can not serve the people cannot rule!

PHINEUS.

Insolent wretches! and what did the King?

MOIRIS.

He ruled his people; ruled them like a King,
Serving and saving them. He gave his word
That he would serve and save them, gave them
    hope
That he could serve and save them; and so stilled
And taught their passion patience, calmed their
    fear,
And gave them faith and courage, that if trust
And gratitude and reverence could avail
To help him now, there were no need to grieve.

PHINEUS.

Aye, if they could—

MOIRIS.

          And so they can in time.

PHINEUS.

In time, in time! In time is now; and now,
Now what do they avail? Old man, you talk.
Their gratitude, their reverence, their trust!

Their selfishness, their cowardice—Good God!
To think that a great King should come to this,
And a priest praise him for it! Oracle!
Why ask the oracle? or having asked,
Who ever knew an oracle so dear
Interpretation could not cloud its sense?
What were the words of this?

    Moiris.

      The words were these:
To save his land and people, let the King
Give up the very dearest thing he has,
One life for many, to be bound and left
Alone upon the sea-shore, to wait there
The doom appointed, between dawn and day.

    Phineus.

Could that not be evaded? Why not call
The Queen his dearest, and let her atone
Her own destructive folly?

MOIRIS.

                             So the Queen
Wished to interpret it.

PHINEUS.

                             But *you* perhaps—

MOIRIS.

The *King* bade read it otherwise, and said,
His wish was not to evade but to fulfil,
His duty being not to cheat but save?

PHINEUS.

To save, to save—why yes! but whom to save?
Churls and their cattle I suppose. 'Tis strange!
But even then, say he had sent away
The Princess from the palace, out of reach,
Then he would not have had her—nay by Heaven,
Not once nor twice but many times the Queen,
Here in the palace, promised her to me,

And she was mine then surely, in a sense,—
Had I but known, they should have let me know,
They did me wrong to act before I came.
Had I been here but yesterday, last night,
I would have saved her spite of all; at least
I could have carried her away by force—
Now 'tis too late.

    MOIRIS *(contemptuously at first.)*

        Nay, why is it too late?
How do you know it is too late—for you!
She still was living when we left her there,
Go take her now by force!

        Ah! what a thought
Strikes me and shakes me with a wild desire!
O, Phineus, Girls, I know not what I think!
What if it were enough to leave her there,
Fulfilling just the oracle's command,
No less, no more? and what if one should now,
Aye, even now be not too late? Prince, Prince,

You teach me to be subtle, think of it!
Is not the oracle's command obeyed,
Even to the very letter, is it not?
Is not our duty done then to the full?
Have we not made the sacrifice complete,
Given up the very dearest thing we had,
Bound her and left her? Can it be that this,
May it not be that this shall be enough,
Enough obedience to the heavenly will,
Enough of punishment, enough of wrath?
And now if one could save her, one like you,
Aye, one like you. I think I see it clear—
One not an inmate of the sinful house,
Not even a dweller in the afflicted land,
One not included in the general curse,
Nor in the prohibition that compelled
Father, and mother and all other friends.
Ah! not to lose her, to abandon her!
You hesitate, you are thinking of it, think!

You have your men-at-arms; 'twas not for us,
The punished, to prevail against the beast;
But you, the gods, made placable at last,
May let destroy the monster, aye, and save,
And save Andromeda! What say you, Prince,
Am I too wild in this, or am I right?

PHINEUS.

You are late, old man. With such a subtle mind,
You might have saved her yesterday; but now,
Unless your subtlety can raise the dead,
What good is it to talk of rescue now?
This is the imagination of remorse,
Too late repenting its accursed deed,
That clings with desperate longing to Perhaps.
Too late, I say, you know it is too late.
It is too late, she must be dead, she is!
Why then should I expose my men, my friends,
To this sea-monster which yourself admit
The king's own men-at-arms dare not oppose?

Is it less strong to-day than yesterday,
Less fierce, less terrible, less sent from God?
I know not what you want with me, old man,
You never loved me—is there need, perhaps,
Of other victims, that you fain would send
Me to a combat that the rest avoid,
Me to a rescue that the gods forbade?
Shall I go anger them once more, once more
Bring punishment upon you worse than this?
And yet, O yet, if 'twere not—but it is!
Were it not merely madness—would I not—
You know I would, though I should go alone.

Moiris.

"Twas your own question,—and your own reply.

Phineus.

I have stayed here too long talking. Tell me
    girls,
Is not the King within? Did not the Queen
Go to him when she left us? *(Goes in.)*

MOIRIS.

                        Is it so?
Is this the prince that prated of revenge?
Or if no cure the comfort of revenge?
Girls, for you heard me, did I seem to you
To speak things merely foolish? O, I thought
To move him as the rising breezes move
The unfettered boat that leans, and is away.

EUDORA.

Not foolish certainly, but hard to judge.
For while you yet were speaking I believed,
But now, like an unwilling flag that late
Straight streaming quivered like a windy flame,
I sink, I flutter idly to and fro,
Now this way and now that way swings my
    thought,
But settling slowly to a calm despair.

MOIRIS.

And my hope sinks; but, like the whirling ball

On yonder springing water-jet that plays,
Thrown off and downcast, it is restless still,
And ever struggling upward climbs and falls,
Springs, slips and drops and wavers, and again
Upspringing bird-like no one can tell how,
Look! hovers trembling, on the very point!
I take it for an omen! Yes—and yet—
O, that this prince were but a prince indeed!
But even the gods themselves work but with
    means,
And doubting him who seemed the heaven-sent
    means,
I doubt myself, whom else I would affirm
To have been undoubtedly inspired of God.
But I will follow him, will once again,
And ah! less passionately put my case,
More clearly therefore, and perhaps prevail.
I wronged him doubtless and I wronged my
    cause,

No faith inspiring because wanting faith.

Still, still I think that she may yet be saved.
    (*Goes in.*)

THE CHORUS.

Is this the man we idly thought
    so cold and hard before?
Surely his love is more than ours
    even as his hope is more.
Yet what avails it more than ours,
    whose weakness we deplore?

And yet strange stories have been told,
    aye, even in our days,
Of dreadful death beyond all hope
    escaped in wondrous ways.
One tale, indeed, how many a time,
    against my mother's knee
Well nestling have I begged to hear,
    the tale of Danaë!

ANDROMEDA'S ESCAPE.

The beautiful, the motherless,
        the daughter of a king,
Who in her father's eyes became
        as an accursed thing.

For having heard it prophesied
        that by his daughter's son
Should come his dreaded death to him
        in some strange way unknown;
With that remorseless cruelty—
        which only comes of fear,
As soon as e'er her boy was born,
        his only daughter dear
He set adrift,—her child and her,—
        a child herself was she,
To drown or starve or die of grief
        upon the homeless sea.

But gently as its mother's arms
        upbore the helpless child,

As gently was her boat upborne
> by waters strangely mild,
And gentle as herself the winds
> were round her night and day,
Still wafting her as in a dream
> along the appointed way,
Till to a glistening shore she came,
> edged with a lace-like foam,
And in sea-girt Seriphos found
> a refuge and a home.

There many a year she lived and there
> still lives, 'tis said, to-day,
Well loved and loving with her boy,
> of whom the travellers say
That there is none so beautiful,
> so hero-like as he,
As he whose early, awful death
> seemed once a certainty:
And, ah! would God, Andromeda!
> lost one for whom we wail,

That many a child might hear of you
   hereafter such a tale!

Thus, as a ship-wrecked man, escaped
   a moment to the shore,
Hurled thither by the very waves
   that baffled him before,
Half-drowned and fainting and afraid,
   can only clutch the sand,
And lie flat on his face and cling
   and cling with foot and hand,
For fear the waters' backward rush,
   if he attempt to crawl,
May tear him off and bear him back
   and drown him after all;—
Thus we, a moment lifted up
   from midst the bitter sea
Of helpless grief and hurled on hope,
   cling to it doubtfully,
Expecting when the refluent wave
   shall, with a grating roar,

Like pebbles whirl us down the slope
      of that unsettled shore,
And sea-ward sweeping us afar,
      o'erwhelm and sink us there,
With all the weight of all the waves
      of desolate despair!

MOIRIS (*Returning*).

It needed a rude shock to waken me;
But I have had it: I shall dream no more.

THE CHORUS.

'Tis hard, 'tis hard, it is too hard to bear
That love should be so helpless: it can bleed
To see the loved one suffer, it can burn
Itself to suffer in the loved one's place,
Can feel it shameful to be free from pain,
Can long to die to save her from a pang,
Can do all this, and this is all it can.—

Eudora.

But who is this that panting and aflame,
Comes stumbling and yet running up the walk?

The Messenger.

If I could see him—can I see the King?
Strange things have happened, I have news to tell.

Moiris.

What kind of news? nay, there can be but one.

Eudora.

Are you so ignorant then of all things here
That you can hope to see the King to-day?
Ah! and yet there he comes.

Kepheus (*Coming from the palace.*)

                        Still with us, girls?
Moiris, I wish to talk with you. Who's this?

Moiris.

A man who brings you news, he says.

KEPHEUS.

       Ah, news.
The world goes on, things happen, there is news!
Well then, whence came you, and what is your
  news?

THE MESSENGER.

Straight from the sea-shore I ran hither, sire,
To tell you that the Princess—

MOIRIS.

       Fool! be still!

KEPHEUS.

Your shoulder for a moment, Moiris. Strange!
I thought I had been dipped so deep in grief
Nothing could hurt me.

      What you mean to say,
Is that the Princess certainly is dead.
Thanks, 'twas strange news to run with, though
  the intent—

I think I know you! are not you that one
Of the three fisher-brothers that escaped?
I see it now; Moiris, you understand,
Doubtless the shock of it has turned his brain.
Let him be cared for kindly. Peasant, King!
Ah God! how little difference after all
Is there between the peasant and the King!

The Messenger.

Nay, sire ; but hear me for a moment, sire!
Not dead I saw the Princess, but alive,
I saw her living and the beast is dead.

Kepheus.

By Heavens, this is too much!

Moiris.

      Nay, hear him, sire!
This is not madness but the truth I think,
The very truth which I so dimly saw,
And could not prove and could not disbelieve.

KEPHEUS.

Well well, tell out your story.

THE MESSENGER.

When the priests
Went down this morning early to the shore
I followed them, in hopes that thus I might
Go and come safely from the fishing-place,
Where many things were left that dreadful day,
Mine and my brothers', which, for I am poor,
I needed sorely and thought worth the risk.
I found them all, just as we left them there,
Nets, lines and tools, and even the skiff unhurt,
Though only tethered to a spike i' the sand;
A little chafed she was, but nothing much,
And not a thole-pin broken, and both oars
Safe where we left them—I was glad enough,
And got all snug as quickly as I could,
And then was thinking whether 'twould be safe
To take the boat round by the point or not,

Or whether I had better draw her up
And leave her on the sand, and go afoot
After the priests, with what I needed most
Slung in a bundle—I was thinking this,
When on a sudden the slow rippling sea,
Till now smooth as a meadow and as still,
Began to hiss and murmur on the sand,
And break and foam and writhe against the rocks,
And gnash white teeth abroad; the while a wind
Blew cold from the eastward, where a flock of
    clouds
Showed red as blood. I shivered and stood still
And looked round fearfully; the priests were
    gone;
The grey gulls silently flew round and round;
The white robe of the Princess 'gainst the rock
Looked cold and awful; and then all at once
Was splendid, dazzling, like a cloud that floats
Close to the sun; and whether it was that,

Or whether 'twas the flashing of the waves
Beneath the sudden sunrise made me wink
I know not, but when next I looked I saw
Beside the Princess a young god perhaps;
With hair like sun-beams blowing from his face,
Flushed like a runner's and with angry eyes;
And 'in his hand a sword which, as he stooped
To something hideous in the curdling foam,
He sent down flaming, and drew back bedimmed.
And in a minute all about the rock
The beaten waters were a bloody froth,
In which the monster raging, thrashed and screamed,
Then suddenly leapt clawing, with a roar,
Clean out of water, and down plunging dead
Dashed spray like hail-stones, and uphove the sea,
All this I saw and knew not if I saw
Or dreamed it rather; and I saw him loose
The fetters from the Princess, and half lift,

Half lead her, blushing, from the rock to shore.
So glad he was, with such a joyous smile!
Not when so terribly he whirled his sword
Seemed he more god-like—But he bade me run
Hither to tell you he would soon be here,
He and the Princess—

KEPHEUS.

But the people, ah!

MOIRIS.

Yes, and the people! And the Princess, both!
Thus is the oracle both ways fulfilled.
Remember, sire, it did not ask her death,
As in our ignorant sorrow we supposed.

KEPHEUS.

O Kassiopeia! Come with me;—and you.

(*They go in together.*)

The Chorus.

'Tis he that is dead, that is dead!
He is dead, it is he that is dead,
And his is the blood on the wave,
On the wave that is red where he lies,
Where he lies, where he moves, when he moves,
Where he moves when he moves in his blood,
Where he moves at the will of the waves,
At the will of the winds and the waves!

And the horrible eye-lids are closed,
And the horrible eyes are concealed,
And cold are the nostrils that flamed;
And set are the jaws that devoured;
And quenched is the poisonous breath;
And the terrible trampling feet,
They move at the will of the waves,
At the will of the winds and the waves!

But you, who were dead are alive!
But you, we shall see you again!
Bright eyes that we thought were gone out,
Sweet voice that we thought was made mute,
Warm heart that we fancied was cold,
Dear love that we thought we had lost,
We shall see you and hear you again,
We shall have you once more in our arms!

And you, unexpected desire!
O you, with delivering sword,
Who sprang to the maiden to save,
Who stooped to the monster to slay!
O you, whether Hero or God,
To the gods you are certainly dear,
As to us you are dear, and to her
Whom we pray you to hasten to bring!

Yea, hasten, O hasten, for now,
Even now in the midst of our joy,

We are tortured with doubt and with fear;
As a mother that over the bed
Of her boy that they brought her for drowned,
Hangs trembling, and dare not believe
When she sees, when she doubts if she sees
That he moves, that he opens his eyes.

(*Enter Perseus and Andromeda, Andromeda talking as they come.*)

ANDROMEDA.

Look, Perseus, there's my rose-tree, still in bloom
And there's my elm-tree, like a lily-flower,
They planted it for me when I was born;
And the empty bird's-nest in its branches—O
Nothing is changed,—how natural it seems!
And there's Eudora, and the girls,—Ah girls,
I thought I never should have seen you more!
O those black dresses!—

(*Seeing the King who appears in the door-way.*) Father!

KEPHEUS.

(*Taking her in his arms as she runs forward.*) Andromeda!

(*They go in together.*)

EUDORA.

We know your name is Perseus, and we know
That but for you we never more had heard
The happy voice that named you. But much more
We long to have you tell us, if you will.
I am a cousin of Andromeda's,
And we are all her playmates, schoolmates, friends.

PERSEUS.

Yes, I am Perseus; and though not by name
Yet you have heard of me before, I think.
Andromeda,—the Princess, knew me too.
The son of Danaë who far from home
Longs in Seriphos for her native land,
Which she shall see, which that she soon may
    see
Is why I left her and why I am here.
For not alone, O maidens, in this land
Is sorrow an inevitable guest,
Against whose entrance there is no defence

Of goodness or of beauty or of power,—
Else had I not been with you here to-day.
Else had I never known you, never known
Andromeda perhaps,—'Tis wonderful.
For see how strangely it has come about.
My mother, Danaë, as you have heard,
Came to Seriphos, and there many a year
Lived not unhappy—, for she had at least
The daily happiness a mother feels
In watching over the young helpless life
Whose flattering weakness is a source of strength
In loneliness, in sorrow, and in doubt,
Of strength to bear, to hope, too, and enjoy.
And I was happy, happier than I knew,
As year by year I grew in strength and height,
And whom I loved as mother soon began
To love as sister also. So we lived.
But now King Polydektes, a hard man,
Imperious and ambitious, (unlike him,
Who saw and saved us as we came to shore,

Diktys, his brother, an unselfish friend),
But now the King, perceiving me a man
In strength and stature, and almost in years,
Began to frown upon me with alarm
As one whose rivalry might by and by
Frustrate the plan he had to attain the rule
Of the Argive kingdom in my mother's right.
And so at first an oft rejected suit,
Still urged, as always, in the mask of love,
Was urged again; and yet again denied:
Till, finding it in vain to wear a mask,
The wooing changed to tyranny at length.
My mother, still inflexible, was made
Close prisoner in the palace, there to stay
Till, as the King said with an angry sneer,
But crafty, too, to rid himself of me;
Till either she come forth my wedded Queen,
Or death release her; or her boy forsooth
Find if he dare, and bring me if he can

Medusa's head for ransom. I set forth
That very night upon the doubtful quest.

EUDORA.

Medusa's head that turneth all to stone
Who ever look upon her face to face!
Alas! dear friend, a more than doubtful quest
It is you go on; and too great a loss
It were to lose you by so dread a death.
Were it not wiser, with King Kepheus' aid,
Returning to the tyrant——

PERSEUS.

                        Nay, my friends,
But I am now returning, having here
The ransom that the tyrant bade me bring,
But bringing which I shall not have his thanks;
Here in this bag I wear it by my side:
Athene heartened me and was my shield,
And Zeus and Hermes were my strength and skill.

Eudora.

How came you to the Gorgon, and O how
'Scaped you unfrozen from the awful eyes?

Perseus.

I never saw them and they saw not me.

Eudora.

Now you are laughing at us.

Perseus.

                      Nay; 'tis true.
When from Seriphos to the Argive shore
The ship had brought me, and I stood alone
In mine own country and without a friend,
And knew not what to do nor where to go,—
All day I journeyed westward, and by night
Still struggled onward; till, tired out at last,
I lay down anywhere and fell asleep.
And sleeping dreamed; and saw Athene there,

Who told me where and when to go and how;
And gave a mirror and a shield in one,
In whose bright calm unruffled I might see
Medusa's image, not her deadly self,
And by her image knowing her, unhurt,
Know how to strike, and striking, how to slay.
And in a dream Hermes I saw from Zeus
Sent with unerring sword, and words of cheer,
And promise of a helmet to be had,
Which makes invisible, and wingëd shoes
That walk on air as easy as on earth.
So on I journeyed with a hopeful heart,
Past Atlas weary with the weight of heaven;
Past Twilight glimmering with a single star;
Past sight of mortals, to the final sea,
The Earth's inclusion and the sea-nymph's home;
And there the helmet and the wingëd shoes
The sea nymphs gave me; and beyond the sea,
Thro' drear waste places full of wind and cloud,

Still on I laboured and still on and on
Till by and by I knew that I was there :
An awful place inhuman and alone ;
There the sun shines not, and the moon is gone,
The white stars dwindle, and a something moans ;
For 'tis not utter darkness, utter cold,
Not dark enough to quite put out the eyes,
Not cold enough to quite benumb the heart,
Darkness that broods upon, and cold that aches ;
Nor is it life, nor is it death, but still
Something between them that may live or die.
And like the place the face was that I saw
Reflected sleeping in the silvery shield ;
And now 'twas deadly, 'twas so cold and hard,
And now 'twas pitiful, so full of grief,
And now 'twas beautiful, so nearly calm.
Long time I gazed upon its image there,
Fixed in strange thought ; and what had happened
    next

I dare not think, had not a sudden gleam
And wavy movement of the unnoticed snakes,
That in the ripplings of her tresses writhed,
Thrilled me with fear, and made me quick to strike
Lest I be stricken. So I did the deed,
And veiling close the intolerable face,
Henceforth a help, and yet a terror too,
Fled none too fast, till over shone the sun
And under laughed the waters of the sea.
How glad I was! but not so glad as when
I saw Andromeda, whom,—had I known
That there was such a one in all the world—
I would have gone to look for thro' the world.
And there I found her as one might a pearl
Tossed by the waves upon the careless shore:
Not so, but rather by the liberal gods
Brought there to bless me with a destined love.

Eudora.

Now we shall lose you, for here comes the King.

Kepheus.

Oh! Perseus, could I thank you as I would—

Perseus.

Nay, you would thank me more than I deserve.

(They go in together.)

The Chorus.

At dawn how dull the dew
Looked on the languid grass!
And paler the stars grew,
And ah, how chill it was!
And not a bird was heard,
And like the fluttering breath
Of weakness near to death
The uncertain breezes stirred.

Now, every drop of dew
That quivering feels the sun,
With every lovely hue
In earth that ever shone,

In heaven or earth or sea,
Or cloud, or flower, or foam,
Or in the birds that roam,
Lightens incessantly.

And now, 'neath the profound
Blue of the sunny sky,
How musically sound
The breezes gliding by;
And sweet the noises are
Of wandering birds and bees,
And sweet too is the sea's
Low murmur from afar.

And doves on easy wings,
Snow-white in pure blue air,
Follow in airy rings
Each other here and there;
Or on the sunny roof
Make a voluptuous moan,

Like the undreaded tone
Of thunder gone aloof.

How beautiful it is!
Ah! surely in the earth
A lovelier morn than this
Had never yet a birth:
Save that, when first from sleep
The earth awoke at last,
And breathing low and fast
Began to watch the deep;

And beautifully bare,
Unshaded by a cloud,
Was not the sea aware
That feared to breathe aloud?
And o'er the panting sea,
And 'neath the leaning sky,
The breezes were a sigh
Of charmed expectancy:—

For that, that was the morn
Which after a long night,
Saw Aphrodite born
To fill the world with light;
And fill with light the eyes
That looked for death, and lo!
'Twas Love that dazzled so,
As day began to rise!

PHINEUS (*Entering after the song*).

Girls, did he tell you who he is and what
This wandering hero? has he any name?

EUDORA.

Perseus the son of Danaë, the Prince
Of the Argive country, and to be its King.

PHINEUS.

So he says, yes; and how then came he here,
Whence coming and where going all alone?

EUDORA.

From seeking ransom he is on his way
To free his mother from a tyrant's hands.

PHINEUS.

What tyrant and what mother? but it serves:
Kepheus is grateful and besides is rich.

EUDORA.

He has the ransom, which he won, not asked:
Medusa's head that turneth men to stone.

PHINEUS.

His tongue at least it did not turn to stone.

EUDORA.

No; nor his heart that shrank not, nor his arm.

PHINEUS.

By Heaven, nor mine, if that is what you mean.

Eudora.

That Perseus saved Andromeda I mean.

Phineus.

And so 'd have I, had I not thought her dead.

Eudora.

But as for him he saw she was alive.

Phineus.

Not seeking her he found her but by chance.

Eudora.

No one entreated him to go, you mean.

Phineus.

He had a happy chance is what I mean.

Eudora.

And made a happy use of it, it seems.

Phineus.

Well, take him for a hero if you will.—
Nay, nay, I am but jesting :—'twas a deed
Worth praise and gratitude ; I praise him too,
And am most grateful to him ; I have cause,
You know what cause I have for gratitude.
I love Andromeda, have loved her long,
The Queen has promised me she shall be mine.—
Girls, we are friends together are we not?
Befriend me now, for now, to tell the truth,
Somehow I seem bewildered, lonely, strange,
Like a man lost and know not what to do,
I missed a chance this morning, as you say :
My grief disheartened me and made me blind,
You too, you all of you believed her dead.
A careless stranger, with unclouded eye,
Saw clearer, acted quicker, that is all.
I do not grudge him glory, 'tis his due,
Nor gratitude in reason,—but the excess—

Andromeda's, you know, a kind of girl
Apt to be overgrateful, apt to see
More than there is in ordinary things.
'Tis that that troubles me.—This Perseus now,
Who comes to save her as if from the sky,
What may she not imagine him to be?
And then how easy too for him, in turn,
To fancy there were something more implied
Than eager gratitude for service done
In what I can imagine may have been
Andromeda's too liberal word and way.

EUDORA.

For shame, to speak of her in such a way!

PHINEUS.

Nay, but I do not blame her. I foresee
That there might be an error which to avoid
I wish you now to help me, that is all.

Eudora.

There is an error but it is your own.

Phineus.

You think that I am needlessly alarmed;
Perhaps I am, I hope I am, and yet
I must not let myself again be foiled
For want of acting promptly. Help me here,
You think that he is what he says, a Prince.

Eudora.

A very Prince.

Phineus.

At least he is not a churl.
So much the better. Open-hearted, proud,
I think he can be trusted,—there it is,
Once let him be persuaded she is mine!
Help me in this, Eudora, and all's well,
My trouble passes, and I see my way.

Do this for me, contrive that he shall know
As soon as possible that she is mine;
She is, she is, I will not give her up!

EUDORA.

She is, she is! She is not, no indeed!
Nor ever shall be if my prayer prevail.
Yours our Andromeda! that she is yours!
Go tell him so yourself, tell Perseus so!
That she is yours, that she is yours of course,
Of course is yours, as like belongs to like
Or as the captive to the captor, go!
Tell him that she is yours, and tell him too
How Moiris urged you to go take your own,
And tell him what you answered to his prayer.
Tell him how long she has been yours, and ask,
Ask him if anywhere along the shore
He saw you hastening to redeem your own,
With men-at arms to help you; or if there

Alone he found her in the lonely place,
Unclaimed of any but approaching death.
Go ask him this; and then say she is yours!
But as for me, if I were to decide,
I think Medusa were the one for you,
She will not vex you with too warm a heart!

PHINEUS.

But first for him who set you on, and then—

(*Goes.*)

THE CHORUS.

Like an obstructing fog that chills
And numbs the narrowing space it fills,
Blots out the meadows and the trees,
Blots out the houses by degrees,
And all the excluded world around
Makes colourless and vague of sound,
And all the sky and all the sea
But a disheartening memory;—

O passionate heart and pure and true,
Andromeda! like this to you,—
Than the sea-monster more to fear
Untamed, unchecked in his career,—
The wasting death-in-life would be
Of this man's cold proximity.

But like the sunlight and the wind
That shake, that send the pierced and thinned
And shivering mists apart, afar,
Till bright and broad the waters are
Beneath the broad blue heaven that lie
With beckoning smiles from shore to sky;
And green and gold for many a mile
The trees that sing, the fields that smile;—
Like these and more, to you shall be
The conquering love that sets you free,
That sets you free, that sets you where
In Love's expanding light and air,

Is endless growth from hour to hour

Of lovely bud to lovelier flower.

(As the song ceases Moiris is seen coming slowly from the palace.)

EUDORA.

But look, "tis Moiris like a man amazed.

Something has happened.   Ah, we were to blame.

What may not Phineus have been stung to do !

MOIRIS.

O, I have seen what I can not believe,

What would to Heaven I could forget again !

But it was necessary, it was just.

EUDORA.

Ah, Heaven be praised, it was not Perseus then,

Just now Prince Phineus left us with a threat—

MOIRIS.

Yes, and well nigh fulfilled it ; 'twas his plan

That some half dozen of his men-at-arms

Lying in ambush by the Western gate

Should silently seize Perseus, by himself
Lured thither unsuspicious, and at speed
Carry him off, and either over sea
Send him unhurt to Argos, if he chose,
Promising never to return again,
Or hold him in imprisonment, or worse.
This we learned afterwards. 'Twas all prepared,
Horses and men in waiting, but so blind
A rage came over him, as you shall hear,
That all was thwarted terribly—The King,
Perseus and I were in the inner court,
Talking together, walking up and down,
When Phineus came and found us. With a face
Working as clouds work in a wind, a voice
Half whisper and half hiss, he first aside
Spoke with the King a moment, and then turned,—
 Handling his sword-hilt with a shaky hand
That made the loose blade rattle in the sheath,—
To Perseus fiercely; and with heavy breath,

Like one repeating a set form of words,
Said something undistinguished, such a strange
Half-human sound his voice was, like a moan,
Only I caught the ending, *Will you go?*
At which the King indignant and **ashamed**,—
*Phineus, remember that, that we are akin,
Disgrace me not before my guest, before
My benefactor:* **be a man!** But he,
More like a beast that leaps and is withheld
And grows the fiercer as it feels the chain,
Drew and ran dumbly, and with all his might
Straight struck at Perseus where he stood un-
 armed,
(His sword and shield left hanging in the hall)
And certainly had killed him, but the King
Caught on his own, that shivered in his hand,
The heavier weapon. At which Phineus laughed,
And—while the King cried *Coward,* **wait!** and
 ran

Swift to the hall to arm himself—said *Now!*
Now then I have you, if my arm, forsooth,
Fail me not, paralyzed before the face
Whose impudence Medusa could not bear!
But Perseus at the taunting words, at once,
Like one who starts from musing at a touch,
Sprang back, still facing him, and with swift hands,
Tore open the small satchel at his belt
And crying *Take it then!* as Phineus rose
With sword swung over him in haste to strike,
(For now the King came running through the door)
Stretched out his arm, and turned away his eyes.—
And Phineus, who stood facing me, I saw
Stare, leaning forward like a bird that feels
The snake's eyes drawing; and then on his face
Fall like a stone, and lie there like a stone.

EUDORA.

'Twas I who helped enrage him: I was wrong,
Not thinking what the consequence might be.
Too like his own my fault was, to obey
No law but selfish impulse ; and yet here,
In the misfortunes of this house, this land,
Was plain enough example of the ills
Which only thoughtlessness may bring about.

MOIRIS.

Hard to keep always are the laws of life ;
The most are careless, and the careful fail :
And thus it is that all men suffer pain,
Their own and others which they give and take ;
For deeds once done are in the common air
To taint or purify what all must breathe.
Well, then, lives he who thinks of all he does
As the producing of germ after germ.
And well for him, whom though he know not how,

The love of others, like a law constrains,
Whether to suffering or to action called.
But arrogance is like the towering wave
That runs and breaks upon a barren shore.

BALLADS.

HOW ROLAND BLEW THE HORN.

"Chanson de Roland." See Ludlow's "Popular Epics of the Middle Ages."

I.

So Roland and his companies
   Were left to keep the rear,
While Charles went forward into France,
   Though with a secret fear.

Meantime the Saracens, a host,
   Lay in the woods unseen;
Bright was the morning—all at once,
   Outflashing from the green!

As many as the glittering leaves,
   From spear and helmet flew
The dazzling lights; and all at once
   A thousand trumpets blew.

Said Oliver, "Now sure enough
    We shall have battle to-day!"
And Roland laughing answered him,
    "By Heaven I hope we may!"

But Oliver without a word
    Ran straight to a pine tree tall,
And quickly clomb it, and amazed
    To Roland 'gan to call.—

"Ah! such a tumult as I see
    Of helms and hauberks bright!
Sure such a host of men before
    Was ne'er in one man's sight!

"We shall have battle here to day,
    The like was never known;
And this that Ganilo knew well
    Who left us here alone.

"But thwart him while there yet is time,
   Sound, Roland, sound the horn,
And Charles will hear it, and his host,
   And hasten to return!"

Said Roland, "I will sound it not!
   Mad were I to forego
The praise which I shall win to-day
   Throughout all France, I know!

"Wait till you see old Durandal
   Whirl flaming in the light!
Wait till you see him to the hilts
   All bloody in the fight!"

Said Oliver, "I know the way
   Of Durandal of old;
I know how stout an arm you have,
   And how your heart is bold.

"But I, I tell you, I have seen
   The Saracens of Spain,
The hills, the vales are thick with them,
   Like grass they fill the plain.

"A little band are we, my friend,
   Too few for such a host;
I charge you, Roland, sound the horn,
   Or all of us are lost!"

"Never for Pagans will I sound
   The horn for help to call!
The more they are, the infidels,
   The more I scorn them all!

"If I am rash, yet you are wise
   And both of us are stout;
And if our company be less
   Than all that Pagan rout,

"On horse-back and well-armed we are,
  And not a coward here:
Lead you with lance, and I with sword,
  And what is there to fear?"

So said he, and to Turpin then,
  The Archbishop, called aloud;—
"Now then, or ere we go afield
  Against this Pagan crowd,—

"Now then, my Lord, absolve us all,
  And bless us speedily!"
So from his horse the Archbishop spake
  To all the company;—

"Lord Barons, here we are alone,
  The King by this is far;
'Tis not his fault we are surprised.
  Nor ours, but here we are;

"And here is battle sure enough,
 'Tis easy enough to see
The Saracens, though to count them all
 A harder task 'twould be:

"Bethink you then, repent your sins,
 Pray mercy of God, and go!
The penance that I order is—
 Strike, and strike hard the foe!"

So said he; and, dismounting there,
 They knelt down every one
For Turpin's blessing, and again
 Were ready to be gone.

So forth they went, at head of them
 Roland with easy mind;
To th' foe his look was proud and stern,
 To his friends 'twas mild and kind.

And pleasantly he spake to them,
    " My Lords, ride gently on,
Here shall a mighty martyrdom
    Of Pagans be anon ! "

Said Oliver, " I say no more,
    Let who will have the blame,
" 'Twill not be Charles's fault, if France
    This day be brought to shame."

So said he, and 'gan cry aloud,
    " Lord Barons, for God's sake,
Hold you the field, strike hard your blows,
    Expect to give and take !

" Together now, have you forgot
    The war-cry of the King ? "
So cried he ; and who heard them shout
    Monjoie ! for answering,

Might well be moved to bravery,
  So heartily they cried,
As forward all together now
  They lightly 'gan to ride.

And now they meet. And first of all
  Was Roland's sword let go,
Bright Durandal, and down the spine
  Cleft with a single blow,

Asbroth, King's nephew, peer of Spain,
  Who boasted his should be
The sword of Roland for his own,
  Fell silent suddenly.

And headlong backward from the spear
  Of Oliver as soon,
Falsaro, the King's brother fell;
  And for a third went down

Corsalis, dead on Turpin's lance
    That ran him thro' and thro';
While Angelier with swifter sword
    The swift Malprimis slew.

His friend the Emir followed him,
    By good Berenger slain;
And from side to side Duke Samson cut
    The Almacer atwain.

"A Baron's blow!" the Archbishop said,
    So fared they, sword and lance,
Peers of the Saracens with Peers
    Of Christendom and France.

Meantime a general battle raged;
    And there the Pagans yield;
By thousands fell the Saracens,
    By thousands fled the field.

"How now!" said Roland, "Oliver,
    How say you now, my friend?
Were ever better vassals known
    Than these to fight and fend?"

So said he, riding o'er the field;
    But his heart began to ache,
And in his eyes and Oliver's
    The tears rose as he spake:

So many kinsmen saw they dead,
    So dark forebodings rose,
For well they knew that morning's work
    Was nowhere near its close.

Outrang the Pagan trumpets loud,
    The dragon-banners stream;
On came the King's own army now
    At head of them Abisme.

King's favorite he, as black as pitch,
    Fonder of blood than gold;
At him, swift on his Polish horse,
    Straight rode the Archbishop bold.

And clean thro' jewelled shield and mail
    Clove him from side to side—
" Full safe the cross is in the care
    Of Turpin!" the French cried.

Then fierce the fight was all around,
    Twice, thrice the Pagans stood
Or ere they fled—too few the French
    For such a multitude.

And fewer and fewer still they grow;
    Berenger's with the slain,
Samson is dead, and Angelier
    And Gerer and Gerain.

II.

Then Roland seeing such a loss,
 (For all but sixty there
O' the French were dead) with heavy heart
 Called out to Oliver;

"For God's sake see how many knights,
 Dear friend are lying low!
Now would that Charles were here to help!
 How shall we let him know?"

Said Oliver, "I know not how;
 No, and I can not, I!
Better than come to such a shame
 'Twere for us all to die!"

Said Roland then "But if I sound
 With all my might the horn,
Charles, who is in the gates of Spain,
 Will hear it and return."

Said Oliver, " And if you do,
 It will be such a shame,
As will outlast your kinsmen all,
 And blemish all you name.

" You would not sound it in the first
 Of this unequal fight,
Ere fell so many a baron brave,
 So many a noble knight;

" You were too fond of glory then,
 As now of shame," he said,
" We are too few to call for help
 Among so many dead!"

Said Roland then, "Old friend of mine,
 Why are you wroth with me?"
" Comrade, because it is your fault,"
 He answered bitterly.

"Brave knights are dead for you to-day,
  And you yourself must die,
And France be shamed; to-day is gone
  The Loyal Company!"

But Turpin heard them and rode up;
  "Cease wrangling, Sirs, for shame!
The horn can help us nothing now,
  Yet blow it all the same.

"'Tis better that the King should come,
  He can avenge us then
Upon these Pagans, who must not
  Be let go home again.

"For us—upon a famous field
  Dead shall he find us here,
In time to bury us before
  The wolf and kite appear."

"Well said," said Roland, and at once
    (Till from his mouth outflew
The bright red blood, and well nigh burst
    His temples were) he blew.

He blew a blast so loud and long.
    Or ere his breath was spent,
O'er wood and stream for thirty leagues
    It sounded and it went.

Charles heard it sounding loud and long,
    And all his companies;
"Long breath that horn has!" said the King,
    "I know whose horn it is!"

"'Tis Roland's horn, ne'er would it sound
    But in the midst of fight.
My men do battle; cry my cry!
    Bear succour to my knights!"

They turn in haste, they ride in haste,
    And loud the trumpets blow;
They ride in grief, they ride in wrath,
    Too far off is the foe.

And swift the streams, and deep the vales
    And hard the hills to climb:
Ride as they will, ride as they may
    They cannot be in time.

But Roland looking round the field
    'Gan, like a gentle knight,
Lamenting for the many dead
    Of that unequal fight—

"Lord Barons, Lord have mercy now
    On all your souls," he saith,
"Ne'er knew I better men than you,
    True vassals to the death!

"So many lands ye won for Charles,
  Such fame for France before!
O, land of France, God save you now!
  We shall not see you more.

"Here shall we have our martyrdom,—
  But it shall cost them dear!
Together then, and such a death
  Let ours be now and here,

"That fair France be not shamed by us.
  And when the King anon
Here finds us dead, among a host
  Of foes fifteen for one.

"He will not fail to bless us all
  For such a stubborn fight,"
So said he, and straight went afield
  With Durandal the bright.

And at his words the French again
　　Monjoie! began to cry,
And strike and spare not, desperately,
　　Well knowing they must die.

GUDRUN.

(See Ludlow's "Popular Epics" and (Miss Leatherbrow's) "The Chronicle of Gudrun.")

I.

Ill counsel gave the cruel Queen
    Gerlinta to her son
Hartmut, who wooed Gudrun in vain,
    Gudrun whom Herwig won:

"To Hegelingen twice you have been
    Where Hettel swells with pride,
And twice your suit that haughty king
    Too scornfully denied.

"If you must love Gudrun, I say
 Woo her and win her too.
Take ships of war and men-at-arms
 When next you go to woo.

"Herwig by Seyfrit hard beset
 Has sent for Hettel's aid,
And Hettel now is on the way
 To Seeland it is said.

"And with him grim old Wate and Frut
 And Horant all are gone.
With boys and women and old men
 Queen Hilda keeps the town.

"To Matalan then, and take your bride
 And your revenge in one;
Gudrun will like you well enough
 When once the deed is done."

They bore her off to Ormandie,
    Her and her ladies fair.
Sometime no meaner than a Queen
    She lived among them there.

But evermore Prince Hartmut strove
    In vain to move her heart,
Till said the wicked Queen "Enough!
    Now let me do my part!

"Here have you served her like a Queen,
    But know you who she is?
King Hettel's daughter, Hilda's child,
    Proudest of princesses.

"And yet what is she but a thrall?
    Now let her learn her place.
To a servant-maid a Prince's love
    Will hardly seem disgrace!"

"Do with her what you will," he said,
  "But treat her kindly too,
Already I half begin to wish
  'Twere a deed I could undo."

So ill at ease he went away
  To war in another land,
And then the Queen opprest Gudrun
  With a hard and heavy hand.

She took away her ladies all,
  Save Hildeburg the fair.
Two years they swept the chambers out,
  And dusted them with their hair;
Coarse were the scanty clothes they wore,
  And their feet were always bare.

And oft Gerlinta tempted her,
  "If you will you may be a Queen."

But ever again she answered her,
　"I will be what I have been,
A faithful love to my only love,
　And I trust to be his Queen."

And oft and oft she taunted her,
　"Your Herwig must be dead,
Or maybe now some happier maid
　Has wedded or will wed:
Else why has he never come for you?"
　"He will come yet," she said,

"And I shall live to see him come
　Though I die that very day!"
"I would I had never seen your face!"
　"Aye, so you then will say!"

A hateful woman was the Queen
　As she left the lovely maid,

And crueller yet she treated her,
    For she 'gan to be afraid.

Summer and winter, well or ill,
    For a weary year and more,
She made Gudrun and Hildeburg
    Wash clothes upon the shore:
Yet none the less Gudrun was true
    To the love she loved before.

II.

The wild March winds were blowing cold,
    The grass was flecked with snow,
And yet these maidens in their shifts,
    With naked feet must go

Once more to wash along the shore,
    So Queen Gerlinta said,
For now perplexed with hate and fear
    She 'gan to wish them dead.

Gudrun looked o'er the windy waves,
    Her look became a stare:
What is it that she thinks she sees
    Among the white-caps there!

"Look up, look up, dear Hildeburg!
    Look! there again it rose,

O is't a boat or is't a fish
    That goes and comes and goes?

"Last night I dreamed the heroes all
    Took ship and sailed away,
At last to take us home again.
    Oh if it should be they!"

"A boat, a boat! I saw the flash
    Of oars, and there again,
Look how it overrides the waves,
    'Tis rowed by mighty men."

From height to hollow on it came,
    They watched it coming on.
"Two knights they are, I see the gleam
    Of armour in the sun.

"I know the fashion of their helms,
    I know their colours too;

Queen Hilda's messengers they are,
   My dream is coming true."

She stood a moment flushed with hope,
   Nearer the rowers came,
Then suddenly from neck to brow
   Bright colour ran like flame;
" Half-clad, bare-footed, washing clothes—
   Nay, I should die of shame!"

She turned away with Hildeburg,
   The boat's prow touched the sand,
Outsprang the younger knight and called
   Gaily with voice and hand;—

" Nay, fly not, maidens, fear us not,
   Come back and give us speech,
Or never hope to have again
   These garments on the beach."

Yet still they fled, more gently then
    They heard the other say ;—
" Nay, maidens, wait for courtesy
    And give us speech, we pray ;
Here are we strangers in the land,
    And need your help to-day."

Still stopped Gudrun. "Such courteous words,"
    She said with sudden tears,
" Except from you, dear Hildeburg,
    I have not heard for years."

Still stopped the maid. The knights came up,
    Much wondered they to see
Such loveliness, so meanly clad,
    Such graceful poverty.

Loose in the wild March winds their hair,
    Golden and long, was blown ;

Soft through the thin wet clinging gowns
   Their lovely bodies shone.

Said the younger knight: "Whose clothes
      are these
   Ye wash upon the shore?
Such washer women all my life
   I never saw before.

"So fair ye are, who wrongs you thus?
   Rich must your master be.
Whose is this land, and whose is this
   Fair city that I see?
'Twere a right good deed, I say, to take
   Such a town from such as he!"

"'Tis Hartmut's city, Ludwig's son,
   And there his captains are,
With eighty hundred men-at-arms,
   Ready and fit for war.

Said the other knight, "Thus always armed,
  Of whom are they afraid?"
"From Hegelingen foes they fear
  Whose wrath is long delayed,"

She said, and shivered with the cold.
  Said the elder, speaking low,
"Why should it shame you, noble maids
  To wear our mantles now?"

But with a blush Gudrun drew back,
  "Nay, ne'er shall it be told
That ever I put men's garments on
  Though it were twice as cold."

"So proud in all her misery,"
  Said the elder knight aside,
"Ne'er saw I maid so fair, save her
  Who should have been my bride."

Said the other, " Have you ever heard
   That once an army came
With many captive maidens here?
   Gudrun was one maid's, name."

"Yes, such a host came here to land;
   'Twas long ago," she said,
" She whom you call Gudrun I saw
   Late labouring for her bread."

" If anywhere on earth alive,
   Gudrun your sister, be,
Now, Ortwein, this is she herself"
   Cried the elder, suddenly,
" Ne'er saw I one so like to her,
   It is, it must be she!"

She heard the name; " And you," she said,
   " Most strangely like are you,

But for your beard, to a noble knight,
    Whom long ago I knew.

"Herwig of Seeland. He is dead
    Or long ago he had come,
With many heroes from afar
    To take those maidens home.

"So like Gudrun do I seem to you?
    Like Herwig you to me.
But he is dead, and she is dead,
    Dead in captivity."

Tears started from the hero's eyes,
    "She was my wife," he said.
"Nay," cried Gudrun, "deceive me not
    They told me he was dead."

"Dead he is not as they shall find;
  If Herwig e'er you knew
In Hegelingen, look at this,
  This ring I had from you,

"For you *are* Gudrun, I am sure of it."
  She lifted up her hand,
"And this, who gave this ring to her,
  In a dear and distant land?"

"'Twas I," he said, and caught her hand
  And drew her to his breast.
No word she spake, but in his arms
  Fluttered and lay at rest,
Poor weary dove, by kite and crow
  Well nigh to death opprest.

III.

"And this is the work they made you do,"
   Said Ortwein in a rage.
"Who will have Queens for washer-maids
   "Should pay a goodly wage!"

"And so they shall! But come, But come!"
   Said Herwig, "Let us go!
Our work is done—we must not be seen
   Till to-morrow by the foe.

"Now let us get the maids aboard,
   And back to camp again."
But, "Had I a hundred sisters more,"
   Said Ortwein hotly then,

"I'd liefer they all were dead at once
   Than take them now by sleight.

It shall not be said that I took by stealth
   What was ta'en from me in fight.

"As they took them there I will take them here,
   In a storm of fight they were ta'en,
In a storm of fight to-morrow morn
   I will have them back again!"

"Nay, you shall have your full of fight"
   Said Herwig, "and right soon.
My fear is that they may suspect
   And take away Gudrun

" And hide her somewhere overnight
   And so foil us after all."
Said Ortwein, " But have you forgot
   That her ladies are in thrall?

" She shall come to you with her ladies all
   As befits your future Queen."

Gudrun said, "Let me go with you,
   Long has my waiting been."

"Sister, except my mother dear
   No woman I love like you;
But bethink you now whose child you are,
   And I know what you will do."
"You are right," she said, "I will wait you here,
   And here will help you too."

"They might suspect your coming on
   Should I go with you to-day,
And you must take them unawares
   And be certain of your prey."

Said Herwig, "Dear to leave you thus
   To me is a bitter pain,
But I trust I shall not fight the worse
   For having you yet to gain."

They rowed away among the waves,
   They soon were out of sight.
"O Hildeburg!" she wept and said,
   If I should die to-night!"

She took the Queen's clothes in her arms,
   She flung them on the wave.
"Two kings have kissed me. Nevermore
   Will I work like a slave!"

IV.

An angry woman was the Queen,
    And would have beat Gudrun,
When empty-handed from the shore
    She came that afternoon.

But craftily she answered her
    "First hear what I would say.
For Herwig I have waited long,
    My waiting ends to-day.

"Why should I be a wretched slave
    Who am a Princess born?
Let Hartmut take me for his wife
    If he will to-morrow morn."

Gerlinta sighed, as if a weight
   Were lifted from her heart.
"Gudrun," she said, "remember this,
   That Hartmut took your part.

" For certainly he loved you much,
   Too much I used to say,
And long ago you had been freed
   If he had had his way.

" But since he chose to love you so,
   I swore you should be his.
I would have killed you with my hands
   Rather than fail of this.

" For I love but him, and I love him more
   Than ever he loved you,
Than ever he loved *me* perhaps,
   And so I dared to do,

"For his sake, deeds to which himself
    Would first have said 'For shame,'
Remember this, Gudrun, 'tis I,
    I only, am to blame."

She sent for Hartmut. Glad was he
    And would have kissed Gudrun,
But, "I am but a servant yet"
    She answered him as soon,

"And all unfit to be betrothed
    In such a sorry plight,
But give me my rich robes again,
    And all my jewels bright,

"And let me have my ladies all,
    All well attired once more,
And give us food and baths and beds
    As rich as once before.

"For, as I am a princess born,
    A princess let me seem,
Till then I hardly know myself,
    All seems so like a dream."

They gave her back her ladies all,
    With robes and jewels bright;
Like princesses in everything
    They treated them that night.

To the sound of music they were served
    With costly food and wine.
Strange was the taste of it to them
    On a crust who used to dine.

And when to sleep they would be gone
    The minstrels went before,
And strange the rich beds felt to them
    Whose bed had been the floor.

But when they all were left alone,
    And all was still again,
Gudrun laughed out, who in that land
    Had never laughed till then.

Gerlinta heard her in the hall,
    As she was passing by,
And, as if touched by an icy hand,
    Shuddered, she knew not why.

V.

High was the morning-star, when lo!
    A fair maid looking down
Saw glistening helms and glistening shields
    Encircling all the town.

Glad to Gudrun she brought the news
    "Our friends are close at hand,
Look out and see them on the sea
    And see them on the land."

She looked and saw the swaying ships,
    And saw the colours fly,
And saw the glistening helms and shields,
    And yet she gave a sigh.

"It wrings my very heart," she said,
  "To see them there so gay,
And think how many a noble knight
  Must die for me to-day."

But now the watcher from the tower
  Aloud began to call,
"Up, up and arm! A host of men
  Surround us like a wall."

In haste came Ludwig, but too dim
  His eyes were to discern;
But Hartmut knew their banners all,
  And named them all in turn.

"From Hegelingen they are come,
  I know their flags of old:
That in the midst is Hilda's flag,
  That shines all over gold.

"And that is Ortwein's to the right,
  With crossed swords on the red ;
And left is Herwig's mermaid flag ;
  And yonder human head

"On brown silk broidered, Seyfrit owns ;
  Irolt's is gold and green ;
And that one on whose coal-black ground
  A flaming town is seen

"Is gray old Wate's, the grimmest man
  That ever lived so long ;
And that one with the silver harp
  Is Horant's, famed for song,

"And famed for fighting none the less.
  Aye, and the hawk is there
Of wily Frut ; and yonder, too,
  Is Morung's ramping bear.

"By Heaven! no nobler banners fly
. Than flout us there this morn,
But we will let them know that our's
  Is not a flag to scorn.

"Up then, and arm, and out at once!
  I will not have them say
That, when they asked for their revenge,
  We skulked and hid away."

So said he; but with tearful face
  Gerlinta held him back.
"Strong are the gates, and strong the walls,
  No victual do we lack

"And darts and missiles are at hand
  In every tower and roof.
Bid shut the gates and man the walls,
  And keep the foe aloof,—

"So shall we wear them out at last
  And see them sail away.
But as you love me, dear my son,
  Go not a-field to-day.

"Ill dreams I dreamed of you all night.
  Promise me not to go!"
But angrily he answered her,
  "One thing full well I know,

"I have had enough of your advice
  Now I will take my own.
I say I will fight the foe afield
  If I have to fight alone."

"Come on!" said Ludwig. Forth they went
  With thirty hundred men.
"The fools!" said Wate, "they are coming out
  They shall not go in again."

Once, twice and thrice he blew his horn
    Right lustily he blew.
With glancing arms and flags afloat
    The hosts together drew.

Ortwein and Hartmut first engaged.
    Both lances crashed like one.
And reeling backward either knight
    Was well-nigh overthrown.

Down from their trembling horses then
    Bare sword in hand they sprang.
Hot Ortwein first struck out and missed,
    Then felt a sudden pang

As Hartmut pierced him in the side
    And called on him to yield.
But Horant rushing in between
    Covered him with his shield

And on his own unguarded arm
    Caught Hartmut's second stroke,
Which numbed him so he dropped his sword,
    And but that now his folk

Ran in and dragged him from the fight,
    Enraged and out of breath
All weaponless as there he stood
    He there had had his death.

Meantime no better Herwig fared,
    'Gainst Ludwig riding fell,
Hurled from his horse, and just in time
    Borne off insensible.

But in the centre grim old Wate
    And Frut and Morung now
Led on their men, and like a wind
    That makes the wheat-fields bow

So raged the Hegelingen men
    'Gainst those of Ormandie :
They cut them down and rode them down
    And drove them furiously.

They drove them backward to the wall
    And there, obliged to stand,
Fierce was the fight to get control
    Of the gates on either hand.

The west gate Ortwein took and held
    As fierce as Wate for shame ;
Horant the east ; but in the midst
    The banners went and came.

There Ludwig fought with Wate and Frut,
    Expecting Hartmut's aid
To enter in and hold the town,
    With bolt and barricade.

But now recovered from his swoon,
   And desperately in wrath,
Came Herwig, forcing friend and foe
   To open him a path,

Till once more face to face he stood
   With Ludwig, sword in hand,
And at the sight of him half laughed,
   And felt his heart expand.

With hope to wipe away the shame
   Of his unlucky fall,
And get him glory and Gudrun,
   Right there before them all.

'Twas not an easy thing to do.
   Twice he was touched and bled.
And when with one two-handed stroke
   'Gainst Ludwig's helm and head

He got a chance to bring his sword
    It broke off in his hand.
But such a downright stroke it was
    It forced the king to stand

Till Herwig got his battle-axe
    And swiftly coming on,
'Twixt neck and shoulder-blade aslant,
    With a death-blow brought it down.

So Ludwig died. And Hartmut now
    With his troop came on in vain.
One charge he made and was driven back,
    And the middle gate was ta'en.

But like a man who longs to die,
    Who yet would die a man.
At grim old Wate, without a word,
    With lifted sword he ran,

And dealt the old fighter such a blow
  Beneath the uplifted arm,
As made him start aside, and pause
  From urging on the swarm

Of Hegelingen men that now
  Thro' the gates began to throng.
Right well the young man bore himself,
  But the fight could not be long.

Sore hurt Wate brought him to his knees,
  And swift, with dagger drawn,
Sprang at his throat. But now the Queen
  Who ever since the dawn

Had watched the progress of the fight,
  And seen her foes prevail,
Seen Ludwig perish, and the force
  Of all his army fail,

Bethought her, white with grief and rage,
　"But I will foil them yet.
They may take the cage that held the bird
　But the bird they shall not get."

She called a churl, "You know Gudrun.
　Be speedy and be bold:
Go strike me off her head, and win
　A helmet full of gold."

The wretch ran eager to the hall
　Where with her maids apart,
Gudrun sat watchful of the fight,
　Both glad and sad at heart.

By the window where she sat to watch
　He took her unaware.
Loud screamed she like a peasant-maid
　As he seized her by the hair.

Old Wate half shuddered, and struck wide,
    Amazed at such a cry.
Said Hartmut, " 'Tis Gudrun that calls,
    As if about to die."

Quick to his feet he sprang and looked,
    And called with all his breath,
" 'Tis Hartmut says it, harm her not
    Or die a dreadful death!".

The coward knew his Prince's voice
    And quickly turned away.
Old Wate growled out, " That lucky call
    Has saved your life to-day."

Nought Hartmut answered, growing faint,
    And with an aching heart,
But let himself be carried off
    To a leech's tent apart.

Meantime the Hegelingen men
    Had all the city ta'en,
Except the palace; there the Queen
    Kept up a deadly rain,

Of boiling pitch and stones and darts
    From many a tower and roof,
Encouraging what men she had
    To keep the foe aloof

A little longer from the doors
    They fain would batter down.
There old Wate found them at a stand,
    And with a scornful frown,

Shield over-head and axe in hand
    Ran swift as any lad,
And 'gan to thunder at the door,
    And soon such help he had

From many a well-swung battle-axe
    And many a well-put stone
That spite of everything the doors
    Were quickly overthrown.

That ended it. The topmost tower
    Soon Hilda's banner bore.
Soon Herwig had his love again
    To part from her no more.

But sword in hand, unresting still,
    Old Wate went here and there.
" Will no one tell me where she is,
    That Queen who loves to wear

Clothes whitened by no meaner hands
    Than those of Princesses ? "
A fair maid, winking with her eyes,
    Made signal " There she is."

"Are you Gerlinta?" "I am she,
  And I know who you are too.
Do what you will. 'Twill be no worse
  Than I would have done to you."

He took her by the long gray hair,
  She neither shrank nor cried.
A single blow was all he gave,
  And so Gerlinta died.

So died Gerlinta. Much she loved,
  Much may she be forgiven.
But if love alone can save from Hell,
  Few folk will fail of Heaven.

A SONG FOR LEXINGTON.

The Spring came earlier on
Than usual that year;
The shadiest snow was gone,
The slowest brook was clear,
And warming in the sun
Shy flowers began to peer.

'Twas more like middle May,
The earth so seemed to thrive,
That Nineteenth April day
Of Seventeen Seventy-Five;
Winter was well away,
New England was alive!

Alive and sternly glad!
Her doubts were with the snow;
Her courage, long forbade,
Ran full to overflow;
And every hope she had
Began to bud and grow.

She rose betimes that morn
For there was work to do;
A planting, not of corn,
Of what she hardly knew,—
Blessings for men unborn;
And well she did it too!

With open hand she stood,
And sowed for all the years,
And watered it with blood,
And watered it with tears,

The seed of quickening food
For both the hemispheres.

This was the planting done
That April morn of fame,
Honour to every one
To that seed-field that came
Honour to Lexington,
Our first immortal name!

www.ingramcontent.com/pod-product-compliance
Lightning Source LLC
Chambersburg PA
CBHW020308170426
43202CB00008B/539